The littlest Coyote

Multi Language Coloring Edition

NM Reed

And

Whitney Lee Preston

Illustrations by

NM Reed

Njla Shojaie

JD Soriano

To order additional copy of this book, contact:
www.littlestcoyote.com
www.stevenspressllc.com

The Littlest Coyote

Multi Language Coloring Edition

The Littlest Coyote lived on a hill. It was mostly sunny, beautiful, and still.

كان الذئب الصغير يعيش على أحد التلال. وكان الجو مشمسًا، وجميلًا، وهادئًا.

O Coiote menor morava em uma colina. Estava ensolarado, lindo e calmo.

小土狼住在一座山上。那儿的天气大部分时间都是晴天，很美，而且很平静

El pequeño coyote vivia en una colina. Era mayormente soleado, hermoso y quieto.

छोटा कोयोट एक पहाड़ी पर रहता था। यह ज्यादातर धूपदार, सुंदर और स्थिर रहती थी।

He had friends that would visit and play. They would howl at the moon by night, and frolic in the sun by day. He loved to howl so much, they called him the Littlest Coyote.

كان لديه العديد من الأصدقاء الذين يزورونه ويلعبون معه. كانوا يقومون جميعًا بالعواء)صوت الذئب يسمى عواء(على ضوء القمر أثناء الليل، ويمرحون في الشمس خلال النهار. كان الذئب الصغير يحب العواء كثيرًا، وكانوا دائمًا ماينادونه الذئب الصغير.

Ele tinha amigos que o visitavam e brincavam. Eles uivavam para a lua à noite e brincavam ao sol durante o dia. Ele gostava tanto de uivar que o chamavam de Coiote Menor.

朋友会来拜访他和他一起玩耍。他们在晚上对着月亮嚎叫，白天在太阳下嬉戏。

他非常喜欢嚎叫，人们称他为最小的土狼。

Tenia amigos que le visitaban y jugaban. Aullaban a la luna por la noche, y retozaban al sol por el dia le gustaba tanto aullar, que le llamaban el pequeño coyote.

उसके दोस्त थे जो मिलने आते थे और खेलते थे। वे रात में चाँद पर गरजते थे, और दिन में धूप में खिलखिलाते थे। वह चिल्लाना इतना पसंद करता था, वे उसे सबसे छोटा कोयोट कहते थे।

Sometimes he wondered, "Is the sky over there still blue? Is the grass still green?" He wondered and he wondered, and he wondered still, until one day he decided to climb the hill.

كان يتساءل أحيانًا" :هل السماء هناك مازالت زرقاء؟ هل لا يزال العشب أخضر؟ "كان لا يتوقف عن التفكير في□لك الأمر ، ولا يزال متعجبًا، حتى قرر ذات يوم أن يتسلق التل

Às vezes ele se perguntava: "O céu aí ainda é azul? A grama ainda está verde?" Ele se perguntava e se perguntava, e ainda se perguntava, até que um dia decidiu subir a colina.

有时他想知道，"那边的天空还是蓝色的吗？草还是绿的吗？" 他想啊想，想啊想，还是想啊想，直到有一天他决定越过山丘。

A veces se preguntaba " el cielo de alli sigue siendo azul? La hierba sigue siendo verde? Se preguntaba y se preguntaba, se preguntaba todavia, hasta que un dia decidio subir a la colina.

कभी-कभी वह सोचता था, "क्या आकाश अभी भी नीला है? क्या घास अभी भी हरी है?" वह हैरान, हैरान और हैरान ही रहता था, जब तक कि एक दिन उसने पहाड़ी पर चढ़ने का फैसला नहीं कर लिया।

He walked for a while, sniffed the air with a smile, and came to a sight unknown. A beautiful tree sat on the knee at the base of a fine green hill.

مشى لبعض الوقت، □تنشق الهواء وهو يبتسم، ووجد أمامه منظر لم يراه من قبل .جلست كانت هناك □جرة وكأنها جالسة على ركبتها عند قاعدة□ل أخضر جميل.

Ele caminhou um pouco, farejou o ar com um sorriso e chegou a um lugar desconhecido. Uma bela árvore pousada na base da rocha de uma bela colina verde.

他走了一会儿，微笑着嗅了嗅空气，来到了一个不为人知的地方。一棵美丽的树跪坐在一座精致的绿色山丘的底部。

Camino durante un tiempo, olfateo el aire con una sonrisa, y llego a nustra vista desconocida. Un hermoso arbol se sento en la rodilla en la base de una fina colina verde.

वह कुछ देर चला, एक मुस्कान के साथ हवा को सूँघा, और एक अनजान जगह पर आया। एक सुन्दर हरी पहाड़ी की तलहटी में एक सुन्दर वृक्ष घुटने पर बैठा था।

And within this great tree, he saw with some glee, shining eyes inside its green frill. Golden eyes peered from among the leaves of this beautiful tree.

داخل هذه الشجرة الكبيرة، نظر بعيون مبتهجة ومشرقة على أغصان الشجرة. وكانت هناك عيون ذهبية طلّ من بين أوراق هذه الشجرة الجميلة.

E dentro desta grande árvore, ele viu com alguma alegria, olhos brilhantes dentro da sua folhagem verde. Olhos dourados espiavam por entre as folhas desta bela árvore.

在这棵大树里，他有些欣喜地看到，在它的绿色流苏里有一

双闪亮的眼睛，金色的眼睛从这棵美丽的树的叶子中窥视着。

Y dentro de este gran arbol, cio con cierto regocijo, brillantes dentro de su verde volante. Los ojos dorados se asomaron de entre las hojas de este hermoso arbol.

और इस बड़े पेड़ के भीतर, उसने ख़ुशी के साथ और चमकती आँखों से, इसकी हरी झिलमिलाहट देखा। इस ख़ूबसूरत पेड़ की पत्तियों के बीच से सुनहरी आंखें दिखाई दीं।

p

And one of them spoke, "Who, who, who are you?" and Coyote sat quite still. Then he said to the tree, "Hello! I am me! The Littlest Coyote from over the hill!"

وحدث أحدهم، "من، من، من أنت؟ "وجلس الذئب الصغير ساكنًا مامًا .ثم قال للشجرة، "مرحبا !أنا أنا الذئب الصغير من فوق التل! "

E dentro desta grande árvore, ele viu com alguma alegria, olhos brilhantes dentro da sua folhagem verde. Olhos dourados espiavam por entre as folhas desta bela árvore.

他们其中之一说话了："谁，谁，你是谁？"小狼坐得很安静。然后他对树说："你好！我是我！山那边的小土狼！"

Y uno de ellos hablo, "quien, quien, quien eres tu?" Y el coyote se quedo quieto. Luego le dijo al rbol. " Hola! Soy el pequeño coyote dela colina".

और इस बड़े पेड़ के भीतर, उसने खुशी के साथ और चमकती आँखों से, इसकी हरी झिलमिलाहट देखा। इस खूबसूरत पेड़ की पत्तियों के बीच से सुनहरी आंखें दिखाई दीं।

"Nay, I think not," said the tree with the knot, "If you were, I could tell. For the story goes, a coyote will show his true self when he laughs at the moon!"

قالت الشجرة وهي غاضبة: "كلا، لا أعتقد ذلك. لو كنت كذلك فعلًا، كان يمكنني أن أعرف. عادة ما ☐ يظهر الذئب إنفسه عندما ينظر إلى القمر ويضحك ☐!"

"Não, eu acho que não," disse a árvore contrária, "Se você fosse, eu poderia dizer. Pelo que a história conta, um coiote mostrará seu verdadeiro eu quando ele uivar para a lua!"

"不，我看不是，"带结的树说，"如果你是，我可以看得出来。据故事里说，小狼对着月亮笑的时候会露出真面目！"

"No, creo que no", dijo el arbol con el nudo. "Si lo fueras, podria decirlo. Porque la historia dice que un coyote mostrara su verdadero ser cuando se ria de la luna".

"नहीं, मुझे नहीं लगता," पेड़ ने गाँठ के साथ कहा, "अगर तुम होते, तो मैं बता सकता। एक कहानी के अनुसार, जब एक कोयोट चांद पर हंसता है तो वह अपना असली रूप दिखाएगा!"

Just then they noticed the moon rising over the hill. Littlest Coyote's big heart sang out his howl for a thrill.

عندها فقط لاحظوا أن القمر ير□فع فوق التل. وكان قلب الذئب الصغير يرقص فرحًا و□هر ذلك في عواءه.

Só então eles notaram a lua subindo sobre a colina. O grande coração do Coiote Menor cantou seu uivo de emoção.

就在这时，他们发现月亮从山上升起。小土狼的大心脏唱出了他的嚎叫声，让人惊心动魄。

Justo en ese momento notaron que la luna salia por la colina. El gran corazon de Pequeño Coyote entono su aullido de emocion.

तभी उन्होंने देखा कि चाँद पहाड़ी पर चढ़ रहा है। सबसे छोटे कोयोट के बड़े दिल ने रोमांच के लिए उसका गरजना गाया।

The owls in the tree said to Coyote, "With that thick orange mane, you must certainly be a lion!"

قالت البوم في الشجرة للذئب الصغير، "مع هذا الرجل البر⬚قالي السميك صاحب الشعر الكثيف، من المؤكد أنه الأ⬚د!"

As corujas na árvore disseram ao Coiote: "Com essa espessa juba laranja, você certamente deve ser um leão!"

树上的猫头鹰对小狼说：“你有那么浓密的橙色鬃毛，你肯定是一头狮子！”

Los buhos del arbol le dijeron al coyote. "Con esa espesa melena naranja seguro que eres un leon".

पेड़ के उल्लुओं ने कोयोट से कहा, "उस मोटे नारंगी अयाल के साथ, तुम निश्चित रूप से एक शेर हो!"

So, the Littlest Coyote howled at the night sky. He turned and bid them goodbye, and said to himself sadly, "They are wrong. They were lying!"

لذلك، عوى الذئب الصغير في السماء. التفت إليهم وودعهم، وقال في نفسه بحزن: "لقد مخطئين. لقد إكانوا يكذبون "

Então, o Coiote Menor uivou para o céu noturno. Ele se virou e se despediu deles, e disse para si mesmo com tristeza: "Eles estão errados. Eles estavam mentindo!"

于是，最小的土狼对着夜空嚎叫。他转身向他们告别，并悲伤地对自己说："他们错了，他们在撒谎！"

Entonces, el pequeño coyote aullo al cielo nocturno se volvio y se despidio de ellos y se dijo con tristeza, se equivocan estaban mintiendo.

तो, सबसे छोटा कोयोट रात के आसमान पर चिल्लाया। वह मुड़ा और उन्हें अलविदा कहा, और उदास होकर अपने आप से कहा, "वे गलत हैं। वे झूठ बोल रहे थे!"

The clouds hid the moon, and the dark turned to gloom, and around him hunted eyes bright. And there he stayed, alone and afraid, for the remainder of the night.

حجبت الغيوم ضوء القمر ، وأصبح المكان مظلمًا للغاية ومن حوله كانت العيون ⬜عة في الظلام. وبقي ، هناك وحيدًا خائفًا ما⬜بقى من الليل.

As nuvens esconderam a lua e o breu tornou-se escuridão, e ao redor dela olhos brilhantes cintilaram. E lá ele ficou, sozinho e com medo, pelo resto da noite.

乌云遮住了月亮，黑暗变成了阴郁，在他周围有一双明亮的眼睛。他就孤零零地呆在那里，害怕地度过了整个晚上.

Las nubes ocultaban la Luna y la oscuridad se convertia en penumbra y a su alrededor brillaban los ojos cazadores y alli se quedo, solo y asustado, durante el resto de la noche.

बादलों ने चाँद को छिपा दिया, और अँधेरा घना होता गया, और उसके चारों ओर शिकारी आँखें थीं। और वहीं वह रात भर अकेला रहा और डरता रहा

He traveled alone till he came to a stone that sat across a great burbling creek. And there sat a creature that had a black feature that made him look like a thief. The thief stood up right there, and said into the air, "And who, sir, might you be?"

سافر بمفرده حتى وصل إلى الحجر الذي كان موجودًا في منتصف نهر صغير. وجلس هناك مخلوق ينتشر في أعلى وجهه اللون الأسود مما جعله يبدو وكأنه لص. ووقف اللص هناك وقال بصوت مرتفع، "ومن أنت يا سيدي؟"

Ele viajou sozinho até chegar a uma pedra que ficava do outro lado de um grande riacho borbulhante. E lá estava uma criatura que tinha uma feição negra que o fazia parecer um ladrão. O ladrão levantou-se bem ali e disse para o alto: "E quem é você, senhor?"

他独自旅行，直到他来到一块石头前，这块石头横跨一条巨大的潺潺溪流。那里坐着一个生物，他有一个黑色的特征，使他看起来像一个小偷。小偷就站在那里，对着空气说："先生，你是谁呢？"

Viajo solo hasta que llego a una piedra que estaba al otro lado de un gran arroyo burbujeante. Y alli se sento una criatura que tenia un rasgo negro que lo hacia parecer un ladron el ladron se paro alli mismo, y dijo al aire, y quien señor, podria ser usted.

वह अकेले चलता रहा जब तक कि वह एक पत्थर तक नहीं आ गया जो एक बड़े नाले के बीच में था। और वहाँ एक प्राणी बैठा था जो काला था जिससे वह चोर जैसा दिखता था। चोर वहीं खड़ा हो गया, और उसने हवा में कहा, "और, श्रीमान, आप कौन हो सकते हैं?"

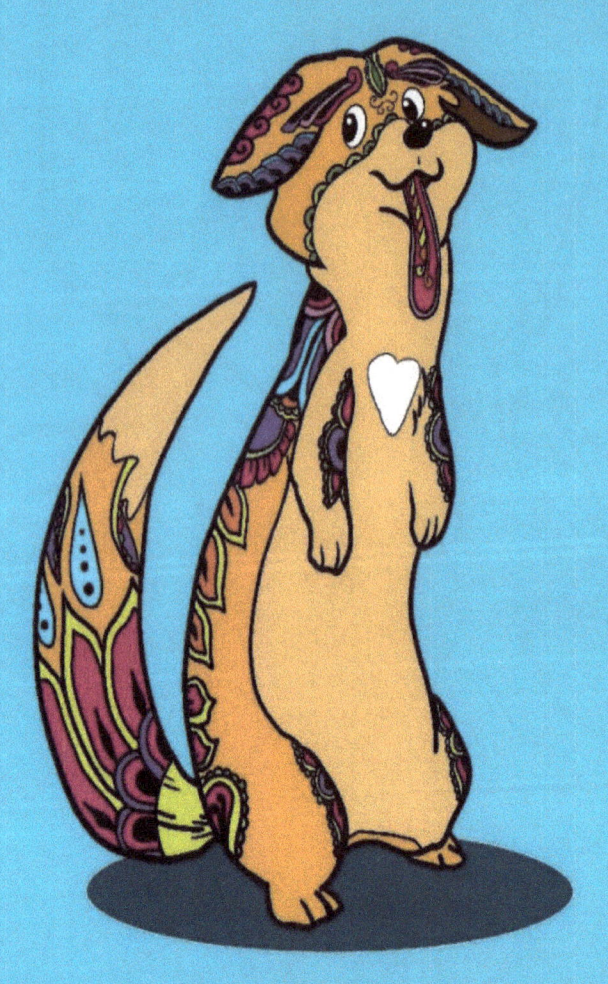

"The Littlest Coyote!" said he. "No, with those shining bright eyes and your long shape lengthwise, I believe a weasel you be!"

رد عليه قائلًا "أنا الذئب الصغير "إقال هو" .لا ع☐لك العيون السل☐عة و☐كلك الطويل، أعتقد أنك "!ابن عرس

"O coiote menor!" disse ele. "Não, com esses olhos iluminados e brilhantes e seu formato comprido, acredito que você seja uma doninha!"

"最小的土狼！"他说。"不，以你那双闪亮的眼睛和你的长形，我相信你是一只黄鼠狼！"

"El pequeño coyote dijo el. No, con esos brillantes y tu forma alargada a lo largo, creo que te comadreo.

"सबसे छोटा कोयोट!" उसने कहा। "नहीं, चमकदार चमकदार आँखों और लंबाई में आपके लंबे आकार के कारण, मुझे विश्वास है कि आप एक नेवला हैं!"

He cried to the thief, explaining his beef, "I am not, you shall see!" So, he hopped the creek and ran up the rise, to continue his journey in time. He himself, you see, did not know what was he. His own destiny he was to find.

صرخ في وجه اللص قائلًا ، "قطعًا أنت مخطىء، □ترى الآن "!ثم بدأ بالقفز على الصخور وركض مسرعًا نحوه حتى وصل إليه .كما□رى، أنا الذئب الصغير بنفسه، لم □كن□عرف من أنا.

Ele gritou para o ladrão, explicando sua queixa: "Eu não sou, você verá!" Então, ele pulou o riacho e subiu correndo a colina, para continuar sua jornada em tempo. Ele mesmo, você vê, não sabia o que era. Seu próprio destino ele deveria encontrar.

他向小偷哭诉，解释他的抱怨："我不是，你会看到的！" 于是，他跳过小河，跑上高处，继续他的时间之旅。你看，他自己不知道他是什么，而他的命运他自己要去寻找。

Grito al ladron, explicando su res, no lo soy, ¡ya veras! asi que, salto el arroyo y corrio hacia la subida, para continuar su viaje a tiempo. El mismo, como ves, no sabia lo que era. Su propio destino quiere encontrar.

वह चोर को अपनी बात समझाते हुए चिल्लाया, "मैं नहीं हूँ, तुम देखोगे!" इसलिए, वह नाले से कूदा और समय पर अपनी यात्रा जारी रखने के लिए ऊपर की ओर भागा। आप देखिए, वह खुद नहीं जानता था कि वह क्या है। उसे अपनी मंज़िल ढूँढनी थी।

He knew himself to be the Littlest Coyote. He had been told so by his friends. So, he continued to tread down this path instead. Sure enough, found it 'round the next bend.

لذلك، عوى الذئب الصغير في السماء .التفت إليهم وودعهم، وقال في نفسه بحزن" :لقد مخطئين .لقد كانوا إيكذبون "

Ele sabia ser o Coiote Menor. Ele foi informado por seus amigos. Então, ele continuou a trilhar esse caminho. Com certeza, encontraria na próxima curva.

他知道自己是最小的土狼，他的朋友们都这样告诉他。所以，他继续沿着这条路走下去。果然，在下一个转弯处发现了它。

Se conocia a si mismo como el pequeño coyote. Se lo habian dicho sus amigos. Por lo tanto, continuo caminando por su camino. Con seguridad, lo encontro en la siguiente curva.

वह खुद को सबसे छोटा कोयोट के रूप में जानता था। ऐसा उसके दोस्तों ने बताया था। इसलिए, उसने इस रास्ते पर चलना जारी रखा। निश्चित रूप से, यह अगले मोड़ पर मिल गया।

There a broad branch did lay across his path this fine day. When he got close it did move. The branch turned to him, and said, rather prim, "You're off by a bit. My advice would be for to SSSssscram!"

كان هناك غصن عريض ويل عبر طريقه في هذا اليوم الجميل ،لكنه تحرك عندما اقترب منه .التفت إليه الغصن، وقال، "أرى أنك منزعج قليلًا ،نصيحتي تكون أن تهرب الآن!"

Ali, um grande galho cruzou seu caminho neste belo dia. Quando ele chegou perto, ele se mexeu. O galho se virou para ele e disse, bastante afetado: "Você está um pouco mal. Meu conselho seria SSSssssumir! "

在这个晴朗的日子里，一条宽阔的树枝横在他的路上。当他靠近时，它确实移动了。树枝转向他，一本正经地说："你偏了一点，我的建议是赶紧滚蛋！"

Habia una rama ancha que se cruzaba en su camino este buen dia. Cuando se acerco a ella se movio. La rama se dirigio a el y le dijo. "Te has desviado un poco. Mi consejo seria que se deeeeeessssviara.

इस अच्छे दिन में उसके रास्ते में एक चौड़ी शाखा पड़ी थी। जब वह करीब आया तो यह हिली। शाखा ने उसकी ओर रुख किया, और रस्मी तरीके से कहा, "तुम थोड़े अजीब हो। मेरी सलाह भागने के लिए होगी!"

Coyote's skin did crawl, and his big heart grew small. He knew this one would finally prove that the Littlest Coyote was meant to go home, and stop meeting worse reproof.

مر الذئب الصغير بالقشعريرة في جسده، وكان قلبه ينتفض. كان يعلم أن هذا يثبت أخيرًا أن الذئب الصغير كان من المفتر أن يعود إلى المنزل، ويتوقف عن مواجهة أوأ التوبيخات.

A pele do coiote se arrepiou e seu grande coração ficou pequeno. Ele sabia que isto finalmente provaria que o coiote menor deveria ir para casa e parar de receber reprovação pior.

小土狼浑身冒起一层鸡皮疙瘩，他的大心脏也变小了。他知道这一次终于可以证明，最小的土狼打算回家了，再也不会受到更严厉的责备了。

A Coyote se le erizo la piel, y su gran corazon se hizo pequeño. Sabia qu este demostraria por fin que el pequeño coyote estaba destinado a volver a casa, de encontrarse con peores reproches.

कोयोट की त्वचा रेंगी, और उसका बड़ा दिल छोटा हो गया था। वह जानता था कि यह अंततः साबित कर देगा कि सबसे छोटा कोयोट घर जाने वाला था, और बदतर ख़राब फटकार को रोक देगा।

So, his paws made a beat on the dirt at his feet, and carried him back down the groove, up the hill, back past the creek, with the thief and his upstanding move.

لذلك، فقد قرر العودة مرة أخرى إلى أ⬚فل التل وهو في ⬚ريق عود⬚ه كانت قدميه⬚ترك أثرها في الطين، وكان حزينًا للغاية.

Então, suas patas bateram na terra a seus pés e o carregaram de volta pelo caminho, subindo a colina, passando pelo riacho, com o ladrão e seu movimento ereto.

他的爪子在他脚边的泥土上拍了一下，学著小偷和他笔直的动作，沿着沟往下爬，爬上小山，又回到小溪边。

Asi, sus patas hicieron un latido en la suciedad en sus pies, y lo llevan de nuevo abajo el groove, encima de la colina, de nuevo mas alla del arroyo, con el ladron y el es movimiento de pie.

इसलिए, उसके पंजे ने उसके पैरों की गंदगी पर वार किया, और उन्हें चोर और उसकी तेज चाल के साथ, पहाड़ी के ऊपर, नाले के पीछे, खांचे से नीचे ले गया।

Old Zora him called, "Young man, I'm appalled! Your mamma must be worried." So, he scampered away, not much left of the day, so he hurried.

إقال زورا العجوز ، "أيها الشاب، لقد كنت خائفًا للغاية ، لابد أن والد⬛ك⬛شعر بالقلق ."لذلك، جرى بسرعة .حيث لم يبقى الكثير على نهاية اليوم ، فأ⬛رع عائدًا

O velho Zora chamou: "Jovem, estou chocado! Sua mãe deve estar preocupada." Então, ele saiu correndo, não restando muito do dia, então ele se apressou.

老佐拉叫道："年轻人，我很吓坏了！你妈妈一定很担心。"于是，他撒腿就跑，没剩下多少时间，所以必须得他赶紧走了。

El viejo zora lo llamo. "Joven estoy consternado, tu mama debe estar preocupada", asi que se alejo corriendo, no quedaba mucho del dia, asi que se apresuro.

बूढ़े जोरा ने उसे पुकारा, "जवान लड़के, मैं स्तब्ध हूँ! तुम्हारी माँ को चिंता हो रही होगी" इसलिए, वह इधर-उधर भाग गया, दिन ज्यादा नहीं बचा था, इसलिए उसने जल्दबाजी की।

Then over the hill, past the rocks and the tree as the sun began to wane. The sky grew dark, at him dogs did bark, but homeward, his big heart did not complain.

ثم فوق التل، وهو يمشي عبر الصخور والشجر، حيث بدأت الشمس☐تغيب .أ☐لمت السماء ، وكانت الكلاب☐نبح عليه لكن عند عود☐ه إلى الو☐ن، لم يشتكي لأحد على الإ☐لاق.

Depois, subindo a colina, passando pelas rochas e pela árvore quando o sol começou a diminuir. O céu escureceu, para ele os cães latiram, mas para ir para casa, seu grande coração não se queixava.

然后翻过山头，经过岩石和树，太阳开始减弱。天空越来越暗，狗在他身边吠叫，但回家的路上，他的大心脏没有抱怨。

Sobre la colina, alla de las rocas y el arbol como el so comenzo a disminuir. El cielo crecio oscuro, en el los perros ladradon, pero a casa, su gran corazon no se quejo.

फिर पहाड़ी के ऊपर, चट्टानों और पेड़ को पार करते हुए सूरज ढलने लगा। आसमान में अंधेरा छा गया, उस पर कुत्ते भौंकने लगे, लेकिन घर की ओर उसके बड़े दिल ने शिकायत नहीं की।

In the distance he saw, and his heart did "Yeehaw!" so bright were the lights of his home. His heart was alight, but not nearly as bright as the face of his child that shone.

رأى بيته من بعيد، وكان قلبه يرقص فرحًا "كانت أضواء منزله □□عة للغاية .كان قلبه متوهجًا، لكنه لم يكن مشرقاً مثل وجه الطفلة التي كانت بانتظاره

À distância, ele viu, e seu coração fez "Yeehaw!" tão brilhantes eram as luzes de sua casa. Seu coração estava aceso, mas não tão brilhante quanto o rosto da criança que brilhava.

在远处，他看到了，他的心 "咦！"了一声。他家的灯光是如此明亮，他的心被照亮了，但远没有他孩子的脸庞闪亮。

A lo lejos vio, y su corazon hizo "yhehaw!" tan brillant donde las luces de su hogar. Su corazon estaba, pero no tan brillante como el rostro de su hijo que brillaba.

उसने दूर से देखा, और उसके दिल ने "येह! " किया उनके घर की रोशनी कितनी तेज थी। उसका दिल चमक रहा था, लेकिन उतना चमकीला नहीं था जितना कि उसके बच्चे का चेहरा जो चमक रहा था।

The Littlest Coyote, and the child he loved, ran and met in the road. He jumped in her arms, and she hugged him so warm, he swore he'd never again go alone.

ركض الذئب الصغير ، وكذلك الطفلة التي يحبها كثيرًا، والتقيا في الطريق. قفز بين ذراعيها، وعانقته بحرارة، وأقسم أنه لن يذهب بمفرده مرة أخرى.

O Coiote Menor e a criança que ele amava correram e se encontraram na estrada. Ele pulou em seus braços, e ela o abraçou tão calorosamente que ele jurou que nunca mais iria sair sozinho.

小土狼和他所爱的孩子，在路上跑着相遇。他跳进她的怀里，她抱着他，那么温暖，他发誓再也不单独行动了。

El pequeño coyote, y la niña que amaba, corrieron y se encontraron en el camino. El salto a sus brazos, y ella lo abrazo tan calidamente, que juro que nunca mas iria solo.

सबसे छोटा कोयोट, और वह बच्चा जिसे वह प्यार करता था, दौड़ा और सड़क पर मिला। वह उसकी बाहों में कूद गया, और उसने उसे बहुत गर्मजोशी से गले लगाया, उसने कसम खाई कि वह फिर कभी अकेला नहीं जाएगा।

She carried him back to his house, tear[s] making streaks on her face. She set hi[m] down by the hearth, his blankets and pillows still in place. Her mother was crying, "Let's keep on trying to keep him home when the moon shows its face."

حملته إلى منزله، والدموع⬚نهمر على وجهها. وضعته بجانب الدفاية، وبطا⬚ينه ووا⬚ائده لا⬚زال في مكانها. كانت والد⬚ها ⬚بكي، "دعونا نستمر في محاولة إبقائه في المنزل عندما يحل الظلام".

Ela o carregou de volta para sua casa, as lágrimas fazendo marcas em seu rosto. Ela o colocou no chão perto da lareira, seus cobertores e travesseiros ainda no lugar. Sua mãe estava chorando: "Vamos continuar tentando mantê-lo em casa quando a lua aparecer."

她把他抱回他的房子，泪水在她的脸上留下了痕迹。她把他放在壁炉旁，他的毯子和枕头还在原地。她的母亲哭着说："让我们继续努力，让他在月亮露脸的时候回家。"

Lo llevo de vuelta a su casa, con las lagrimas haciendo rayas en su cara Lo dejo junto a la chimenea, con las mantas y la almohada todavia en su sitio. Su madre lloraba, seguia trantando de mantenerlo en casa cuando la luna asomaba su rostro.

वह उसे वापस अपने घर ले गई, उसके चेहरे पर आँसू की लकीरें थीं। उसने उसे चूल्हा, उसके कंबल और तकिए के पास रखा। उसकी माँ रो रही थी, "जब चाँद अपना चेहरा दिखाए तो उसे घर में रखने की कोशिश करते हैं।"

The Littlest Coyote lived on a hill. And thanks to his wild animal friends, he lives there still.

عاش الذئب الصغير على أحد التلال .وبفضل أصدقائه من الحيوانات البرية، لا يزال يعيش هناك

O Coiote menor morava em uma colina. E graças aos seus amigos animais selvagens, ele ainda vive lá.

最小的土狼住在一座山上。多亏了他的野生动物朋友，他现在还住在那里。

El pequeño coyote vive en una colina. Y gracias a sus amigos animales salvajes, todavia vive alli.

सबसे छोटा कोयोट एक पहाड़ी पर रहता था। और अपने जंगली जानवरों के दोस्तों के लिए धन्यवाद, वह अभी भी वहां रहता है।

Dedicated to

Champion "Chompers" Corgi

Rest in peace,

my sweet little monster.

with lots of animals and books.

The Dueling Wizards of Simpletown : Pt 1 The Worrisome War of the Whimsical Wizards

Dungeons for Dollars: Wizards 2

The Glass Planet series SciFi Horror

Slander Me Tender Gaslight My Life

Home Is Where the Horse Is: surviving the Jackson Butte Fire 2015

A Safer Place to Be: True story of Fire Survival, a girl and her horses

Wind In My Mane 1, and 2: Endurance Ride Stories

What's It Gonna Be, Captain?

The Oak Grove of Maeve: Cupped Hands, Magic Tears

The Adventures of Elf and Troll: The Two Kingdoms

The Saga of Elf and Troll: The Tattered Unicorn

The Littlest Coyote series of illustrated children's stories and coloring books

NMReedBooks.com

NMReedAuthor.com

StevensPressLLC.com

Walmart.com

Barnes&Noble online

and on social media by book title and author